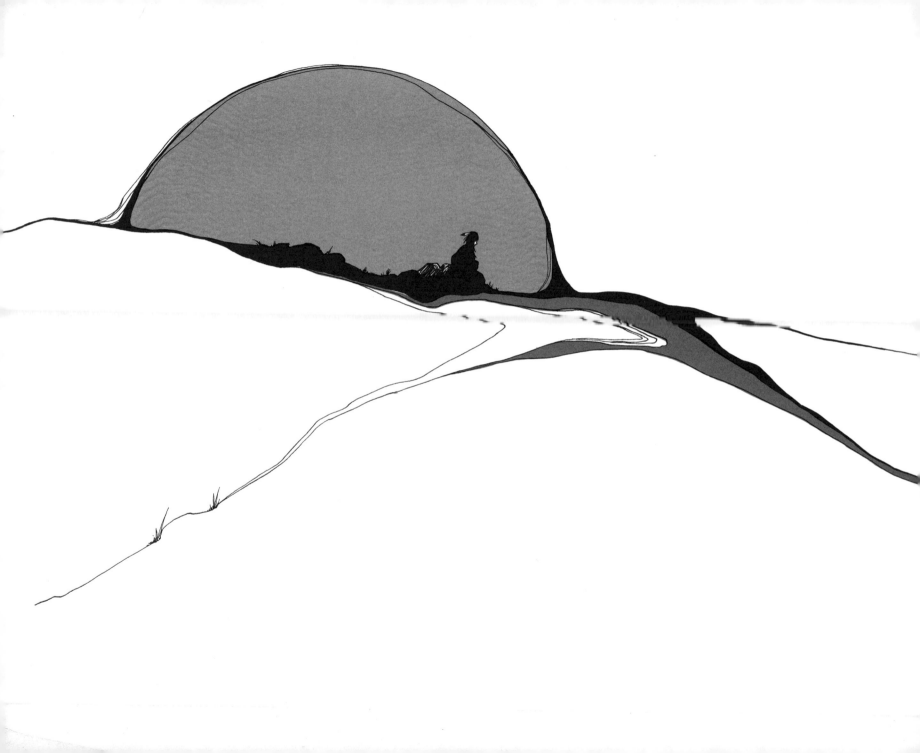

EVERYBODY NEEDS A ROCK

by Byrd Baylor with pictures by Peter Parnall

CHARLES SCRIBNER'S SONS, NEW YORK

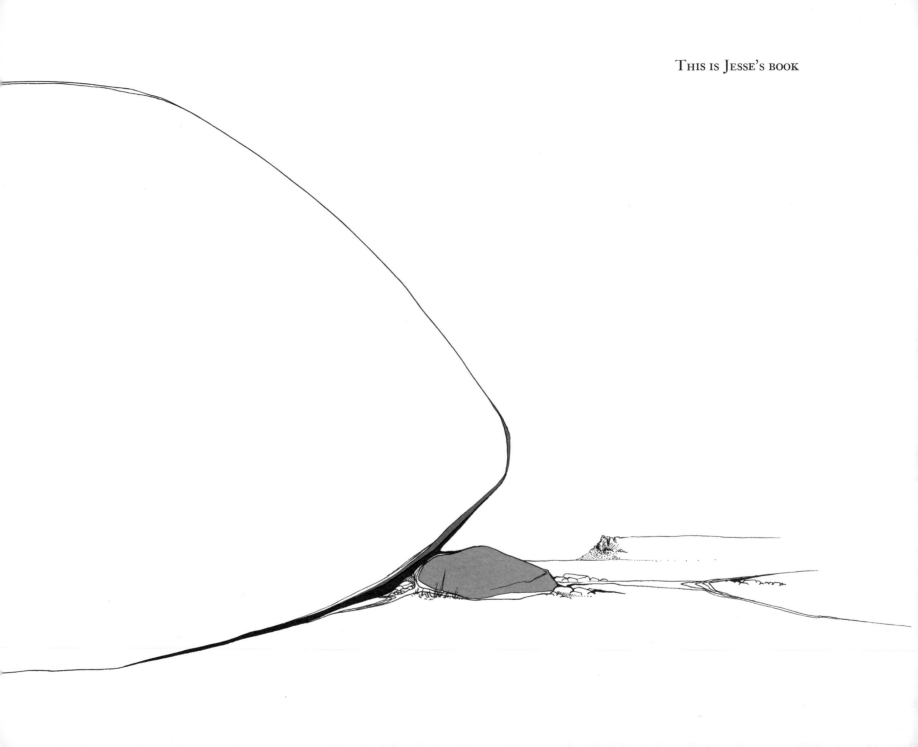

Everybody
needs
a rock.

I'm sorry for kids
who don't have
a rock
for a friend.

I'm sorry for kids
who only have
TRICYCLES
BICYCLES
HORSES
ELEPHANTS
GOLDFISH
THREE-ROOM PLAYHOUSES
FIRE ENGINES
WIND-UP DRAGONS
AND THINGS LIKE THAT —
if
they don't have
a
rock
for a friend.

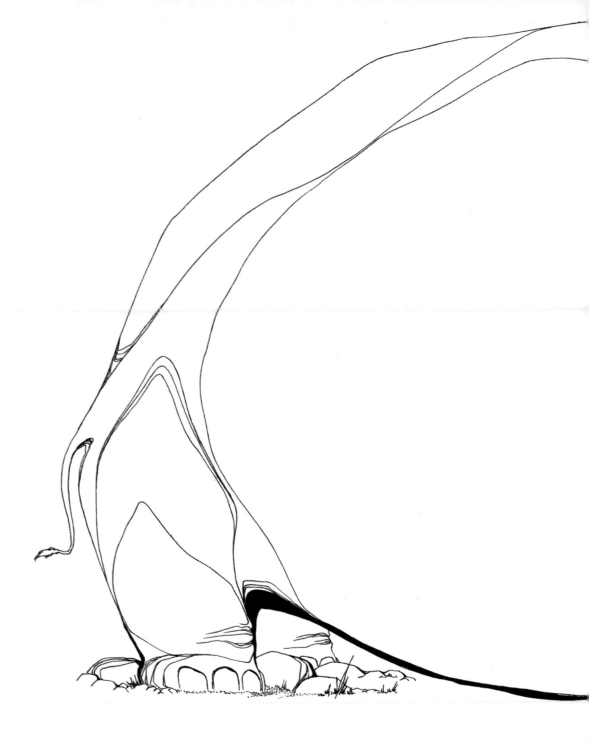

That's why
I'm giving them
my own
TEN RULES
for
finding
a
rock. . . .

Not
just
any rock.
I mean
a
special
rock
that you find
yourself
and keep
as long as
you can —
maybe
forever.

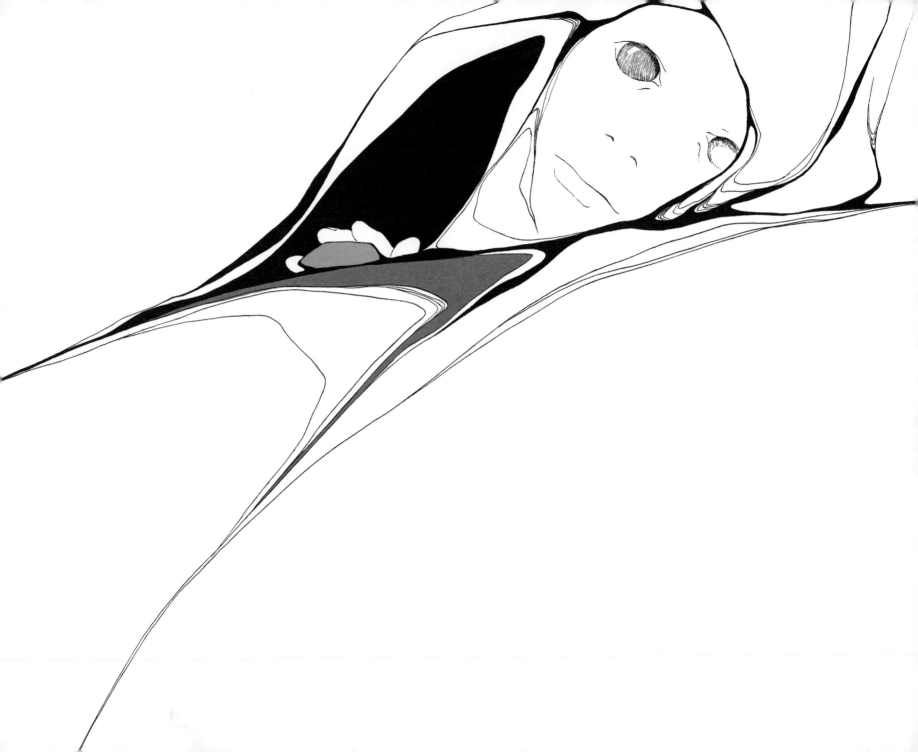

If somebody says,
"What's so special
about that rock?"
don't even tell them.
I don't.

Nobody
is supposed
to know
what's special
about
another person's
rock.

All right.
Here
are
the
rules:

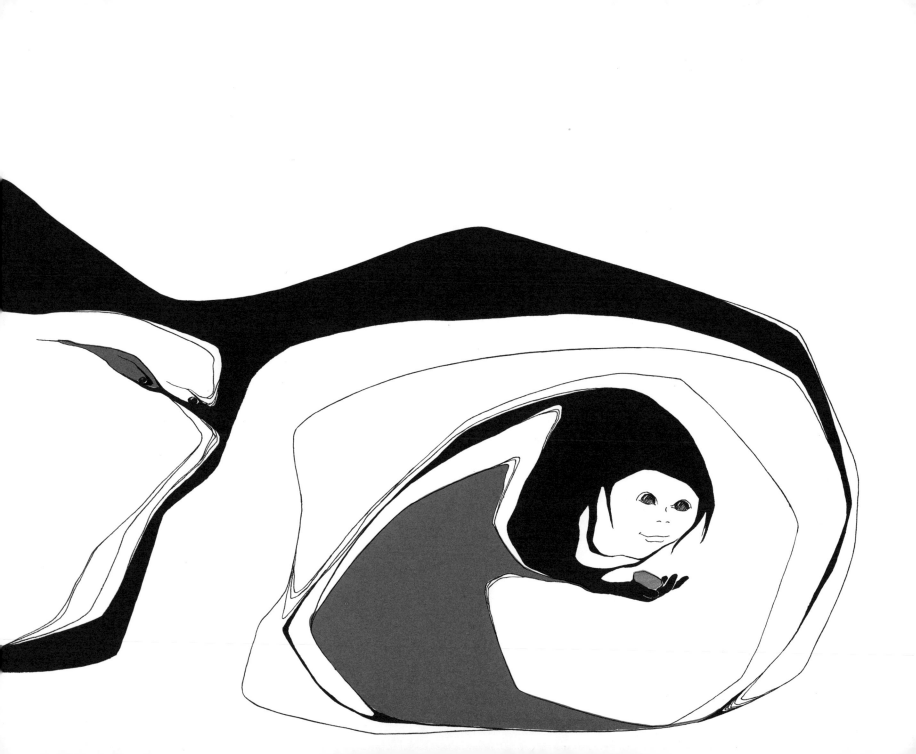

If you can,
go to a mountain
made out of
nothing but
a hundred million
small
shiny
beautiful
roundish
rocks.

But if you can't,
anyplace will do.
Even an alley.
Even a sandy road.

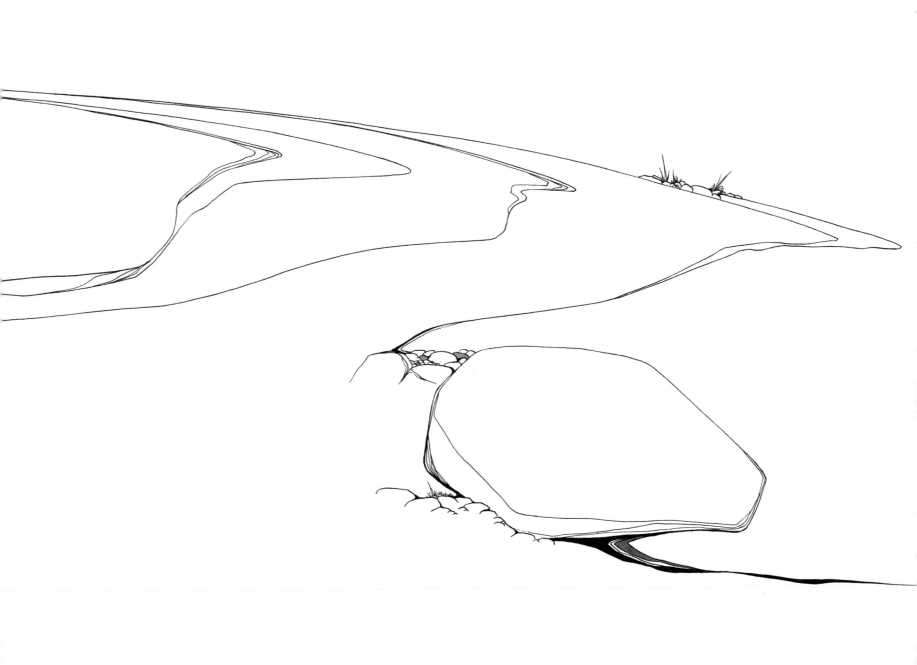

RULE NUMBER 2

When you are looking
at rocks
don't let
mothers or fathers
or sisters or brothers
or even best friends
talk
to you.
You should choose
a rock
when everything
is quiet.
Don't let dogs bark
at you
or bees buzz
at you.

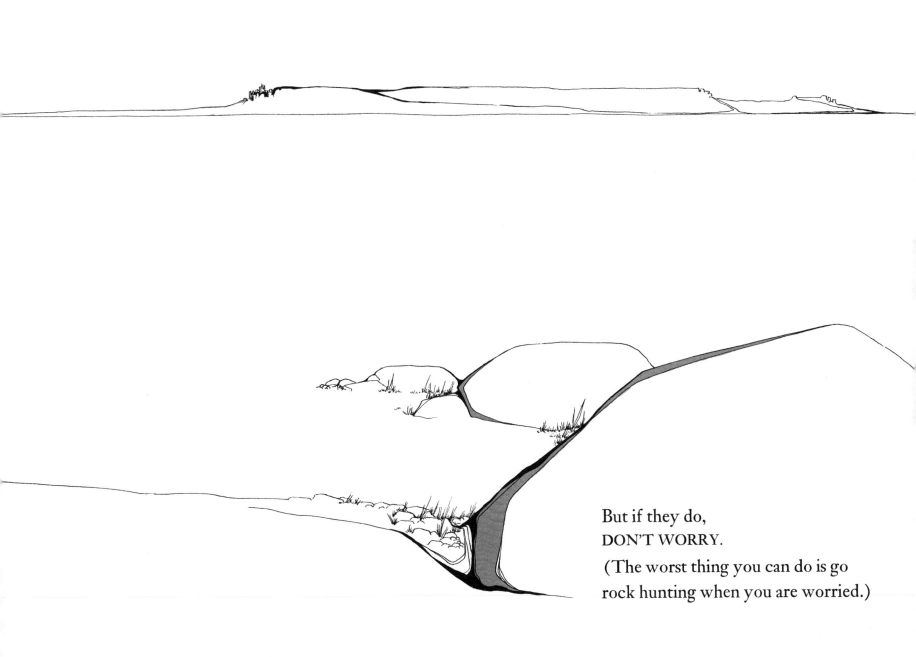

But if they do,
DON'T WORRY.
(The worst thing you can do is go
rock hunting when you are worried.)

RULE NUMBER 3

Bend over.
More.
Even more.
You may have to
sit
on the ground
with your head
almost
touching
the earth.
You have to look
a rock
right
in the eye.

Otherwise,
don't blame me
if you
can't find
a good one.

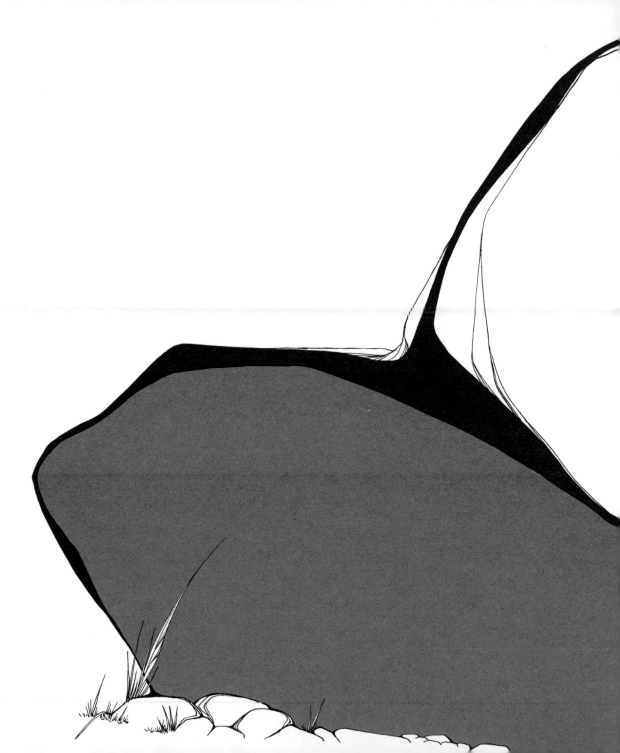

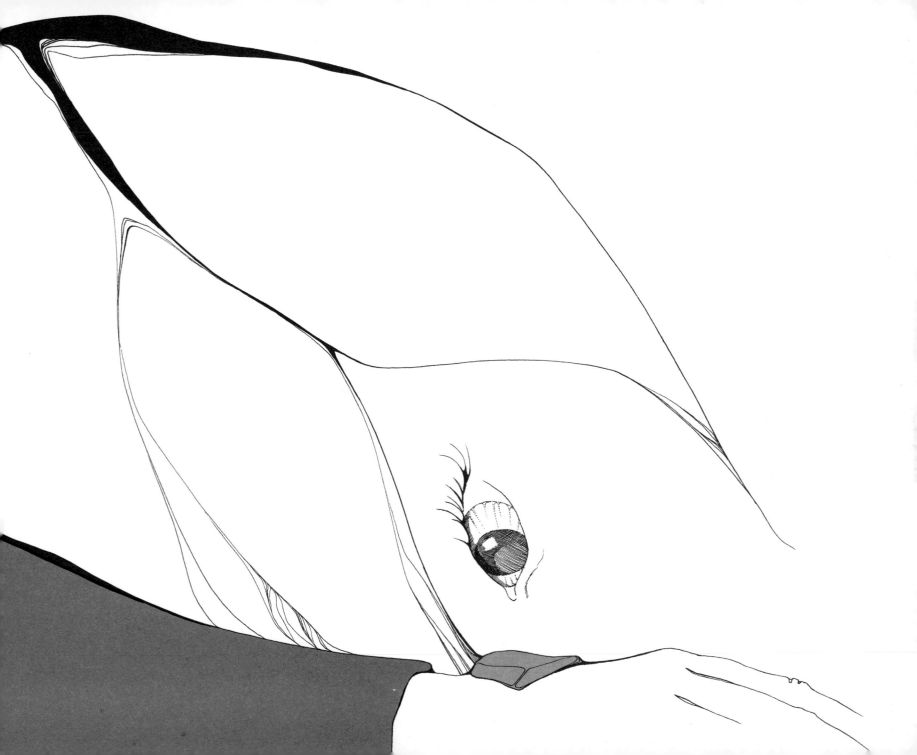

Don't get a rock
that is
too big.
You'll
always
be sorry.
It won't fit
your hand
right
and it won't fit
your pocket.

A rock as big as
an apple
is too big.
A rock as big as
a horse
is
MUCH
too big.

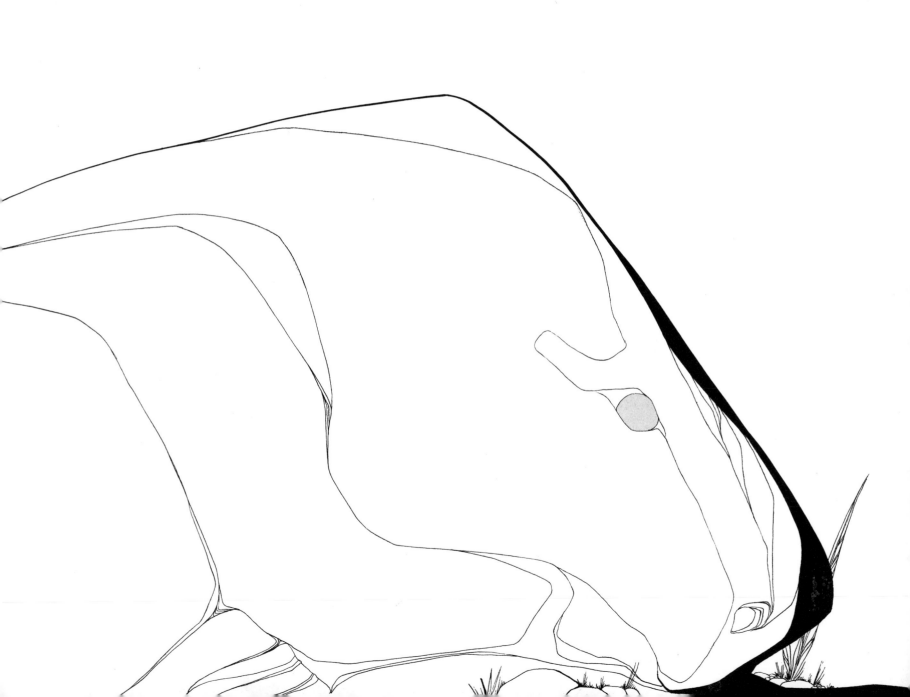

Don't choose a rock
that is
too small.
It will only be
easy
to lose
or
a mouse
might eat it,
thinking
that it
is a seed.

(Believe me,
that happened
to a boy
in the state
of Arizona.)

The size
must be
perfect.
It has to feel
easy
in your hand
when you close
your fingers
over it.
It has to feel
jumpy
in your pocket
when you run.

Some people
touch
a rock
a thousand times
a day.
There aren't many things
that feel
as good as a rock —
if the rock
is
perfect.

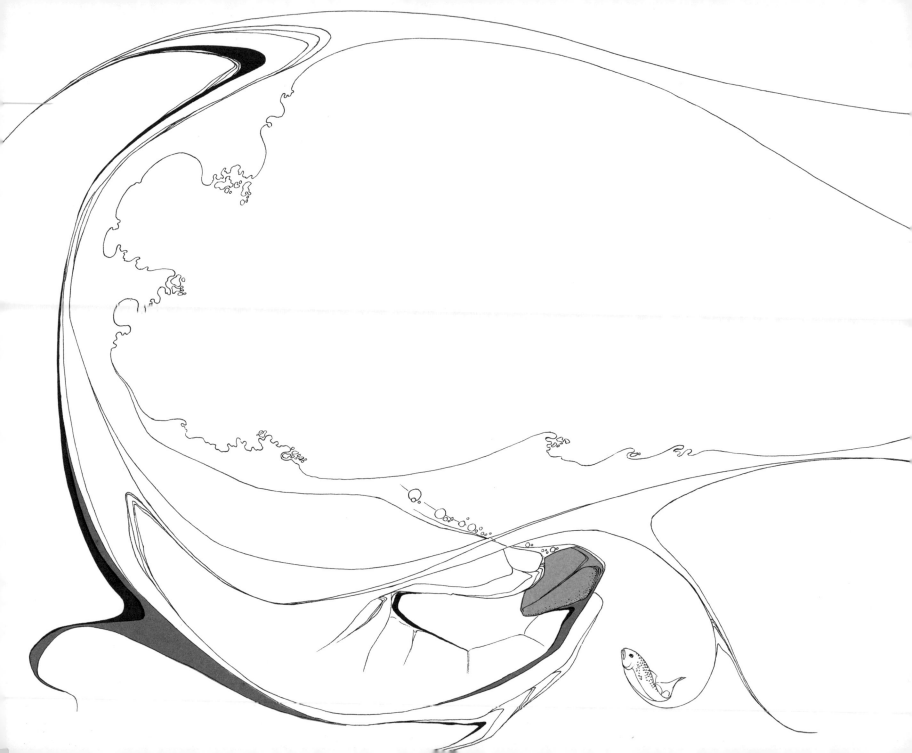

RULE NUMBER 7

Look for
the perfect
color.
That could be
a sort of
pinkish gray
with bits of
silvery shine in it.
Some rocks
that look brown
are really other
colors,
but
you only see them
when you squint
and when the sun
is right.

Another way
to see colors
is to dip
your rock
in a clear mountain stream —
if one is passing by.

The shape
of the rock
is up to you.
(There is a girl in Alaska
who only likes flat rocks.
Don't ask me why.
I like them lumpy.)

The thing to remember
about shapes
is this:
Any rock
looks good
with a hundred other rocks
around it on a hill.
But
if your rock
is going to be special
it should look good
by itself
in the bathtub.

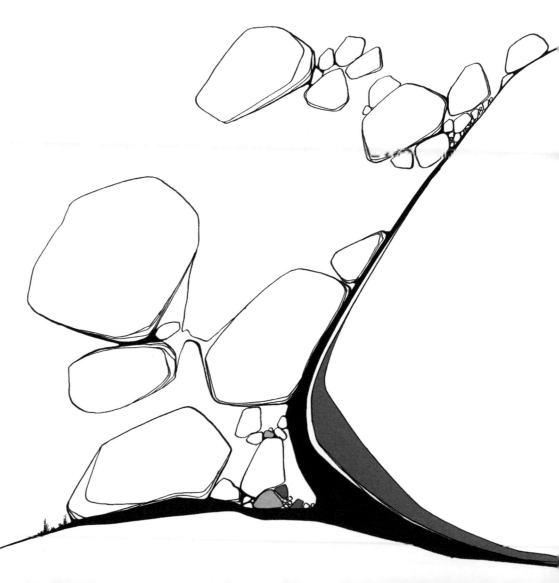

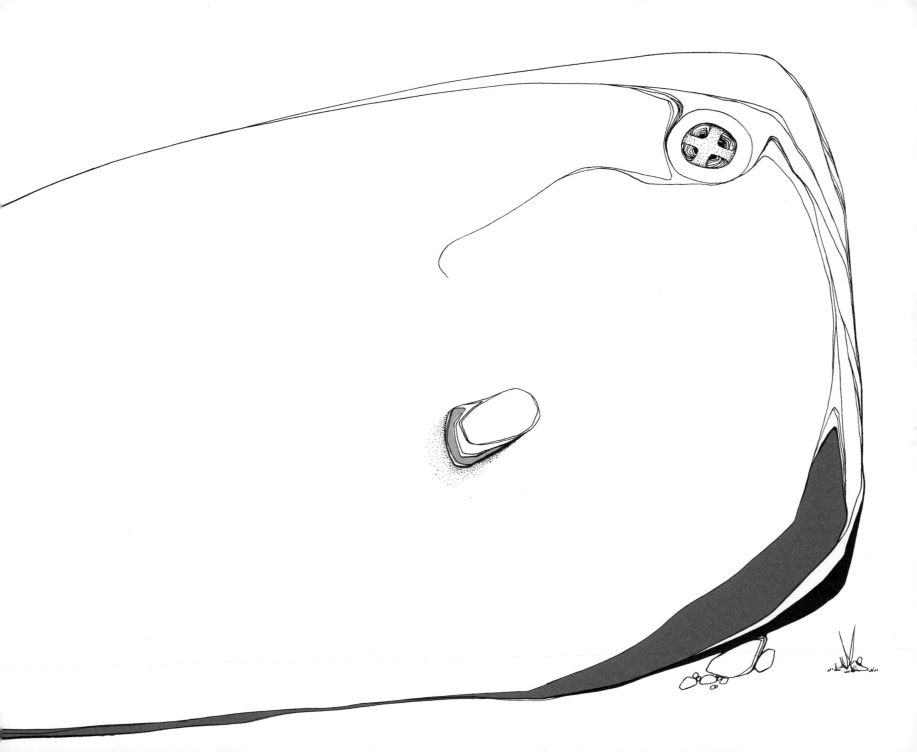

RULE NUMBER 9

Always
sniff
a rock.
Rocks have
their own smells.
Some kids can tell
by sniffing
whether a rock
came from the middle
of the earth
or from an ocean
or from a mountain
where wind and sun
touched it
every day
for a million years.

You'll find out that grown-ups
can't tell these things.
Too bad for them.
They just can't smell as well
as kids can.

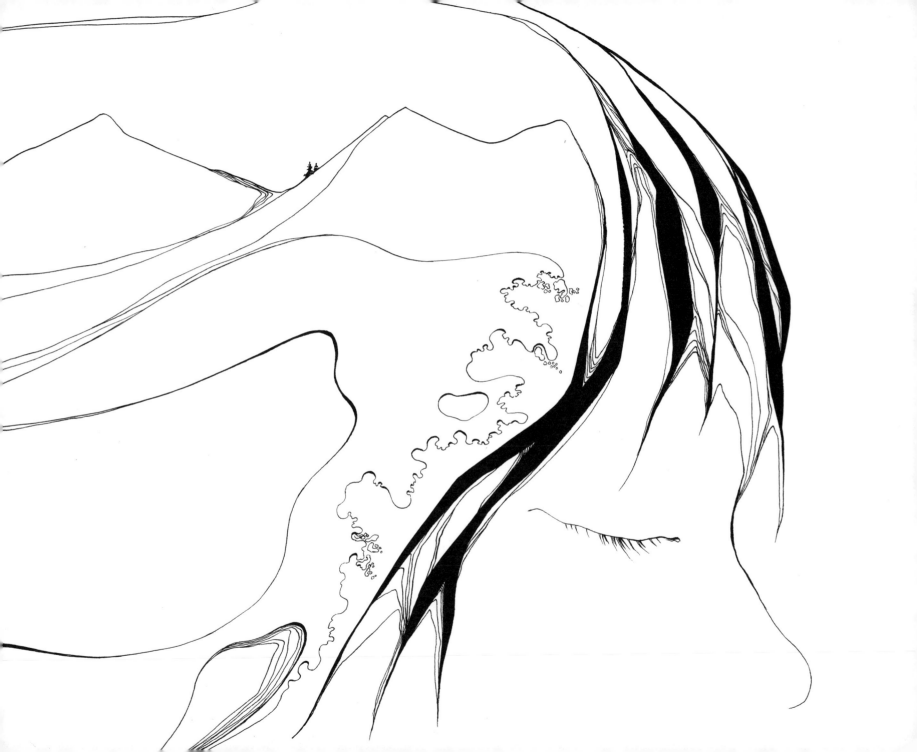

RULE NUMBER 10

Don't ask anybody
to help you choose.

I've seen
a lizard
pick one rock
out of
a desert full
of rocks
and go sit there
alone.
I've seen
a snail
pass up
twenty rocks
and spend all day
getting to
the one
it wanted.

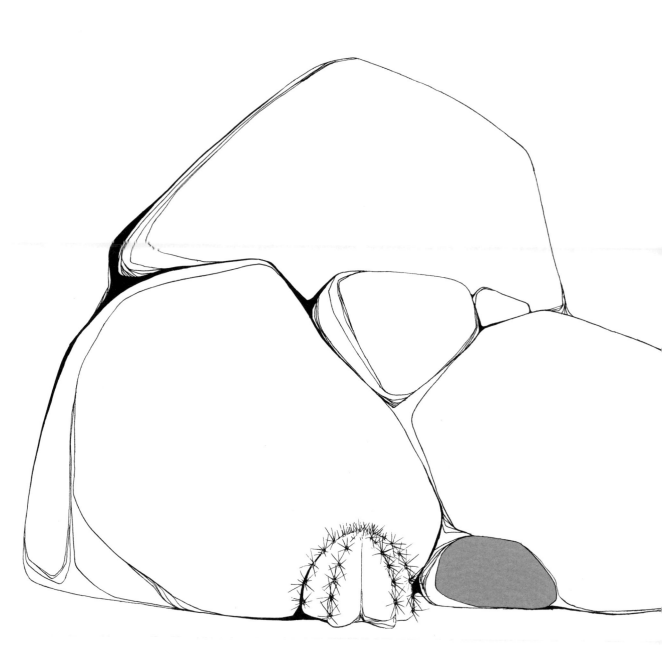

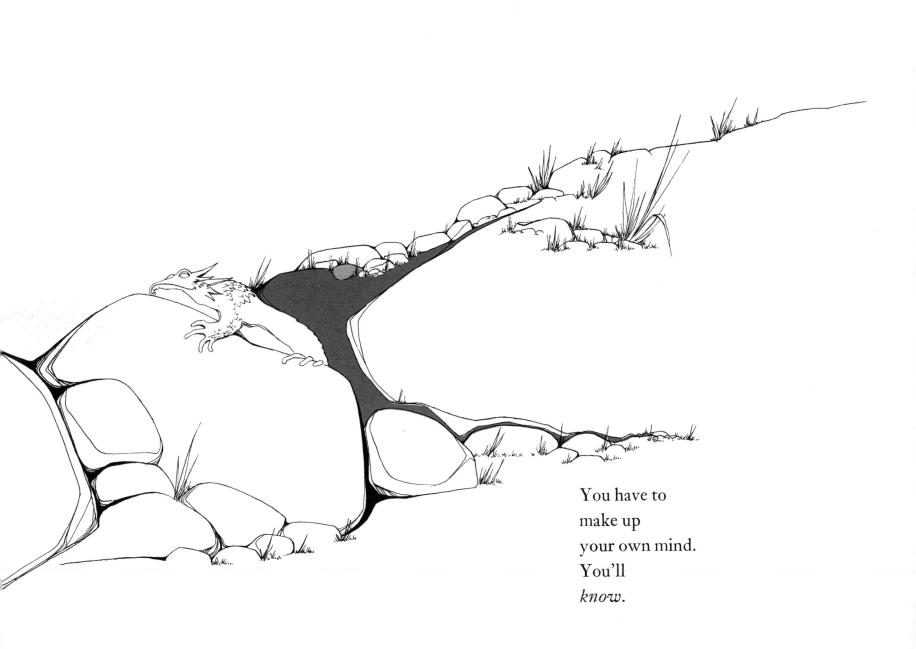

You have to
make up
your own mind.
You'll
know.

All right,
that's
ten rules.
If you think
of any more
write them down
yourself.
I'm going out
to play a game
that takes
just me
and one rock
to play.

I happen to have
a rock here in my hand . . .